True Cost of Wasting vs. Overspending:

A Guide to Smart Financial Choices

Avan B. Maamo

Ukiyoto Publishing

All global publishing rights are held by

Ukiyoto Publishing

Published in 2025

Content Copyright © Avan B. Maamo

ISBN 9789367955260

All rights reserved.
No part of this publication may be reproduced, transmitted, or stored in a retrieval system, in any form by any means, electronic, mechanical, photocopying, recording or otherwise, without the prior permission of the publisher.

The moral rights of the author have been asserted.

This book is sold subject to the condition that it shall not by way of trade or otherwise, be lent, resold, hired out or otherwise circulated, without the publisher's prior consent, in any form of binding or cover other than that in which it is published.

www.ukiyoto.com

Dedication

This book is dedicated to the countless individuals who have been affected by the devastating consequences of wasting and overspending resources. Your stories of hardship and resilience have inspired me to write this book and to advocate for greater awareness and action on this important issue

I would like to express my sincere gratitude to the following people and organizations:

* My family and friends, whose unwavering support and encouragement have made this book possible.
* The researchers and experts who have shared their knowledge and insights with me.
* The organizations and individuals who are working to address the issue of wasting and overspending.

Finally, I would like to acknowledge the importance of taking action to reduce our waste and overspending. Through making conscious choices about how we consume and utilize resources, we can help to create a more sustainable future for ourselves and for generations to come.

Contents

Introduction	1
Defining Wasting and Overspending	5
Psychological Factors	6
Identifying Wasteful Spending	10
Impact on Financial Health	12
Case Studies	13
Understanding Overspending	17
Consequences of Overspending	20
Case Studies	22
Chapter 4	25
Identifying Personal Spending Traps	25
Common Spending Traps	26
Self-Assessment Tools	28
Chapter 5	33
Strategies to Combat Wastefulness	33
Mindful Spending Techniques	33
Tools and Apps for Tracking Expenses	38
Chapter 6	41
Strategies to Control Overspending	41
Creating a Sustainable Budget	42
Setting Financial Goals	45
Understanding Marketing Strategies	49
Educating Yourself on Value vs. Price	52
Establishing Routines for Financial Success	56

The Importance of Accountability	59
Chapter 9	61
Case Studies and Success Stories	62
Real-Life Transformations	62
Conclusion	68
Appendices	71
A. Resources for Further Reading	71
B. Worksheets and Templates	73
About the Author	*76*

Introduction

In an increasingly complex financial landscape, the ability to make informed and strategic financial decisions is more important than ever. *"True Cost of Wasting vs. Overspending: A Guide to Smart Financial Choices"* aims to dissect two prevalent issues that can significantly impact personal and household finances: wasting money and overspending. This book is designed to serve as a comprehensive resource for individuals seeking to understand these concepts, recognize their implications, and adopt smarter financial habits.

Purpose of the Book

The primary purpose of this book is to enable readers with the knowledge and tools necessary to identify and address the issues of wasting and overspending in their daily lives. While many people may recognize that these behaviors exist, they often lack a clear understanding of their long-term effects on financial well-being. Wasting money typically involves spending on items or services that provide little to no value, while overspending refers to exceeding one's budget, often leading to debt and financial stress.

By exploring these concepts in depth, this book aims to equip readers with practical strategies for recognizing and mitigating wasteful spending and overspending behaviors. The goal is not only to help individuals save money but also to foster a mindset that prioritizes value over impulse or convenience.

Understanding the true cost of wasting and overspending is essential for several reasons. First, both behaviors can lead to significant financial losses that accumulate over time. For instance, wasteful spending on unused subscriptions or impulse purchases can drain resources that could have been allocated toward savings or investments. According to economic principles, every dollar spent unwisely is a dollar that cannot be used for more productive purposes, such as building an emergency fund or investing in education.

Moreover, in today's consumer driven society, marketing tactics frequently encourage excessive spending and wastefulness. Many individuals find themselves caught in cycles of consumption without fully grasping the long-term consequences of their choices. For example, purchasing convenience foods may save time but often comes at a premium price without providing corresponding benefits. By understanding these behaviors, readers can develop a more mindful approach to spending that aligns with their financial goals.

The relevance of this book is magnified by the current economic climate, which is marked by rising inflation rates, fluctuating job markets, and increasing living costs. Many households are facing unprecedented challenges as they crossed these complexities. The

Bank of Thailand underscore on the importance of avoiding over-indebtedness from unnecessary consumption spending, emphasizing the need for individuals to be vigilant about their financial habits.

Additionally, technological advancement have transformed how consumers engage with money. Online shopping platforms and subscription services have made it easier than ever to fall into traps of wasting and overspending. Without a clear apprehension of personal finance principles, individuals may find themselves struggling to meet basic needs due to excessive spending on non-essential items.

In light of these obstacles, making informed financial choices becomes paramount. By differentiating between necessary expenses and wasteful spending, individuals can maintain greater control over their finances and work toward achieving their long-term goals. The ability to recognize when spending is becoming wasteful or excessive can lead not only to improved financial health but also to enhanced quality of life.

Chapter 1
Understanding Financial Behaviors

In the realm of personal finance, recognizing the behaviors that drive our spending habits is imperative for achieving financial stability and success. This chapter probes into two significant concepts: *wasting money* and *overspending*. Defining these terms, exploring their psychological underpinnings, and examining how they manifest in daily life, readers will obtain valuable insights into their financial behaviors and learn how to foster healthier spending habits.

Defining Wasting and Overspending

Wasting Money. This refers to expenditures that yield little to no value or benefit. This can take many forms, such as purchasing items that are never used, paying for subscriptions that go unused, or opting for convenience products that are overpriced. For example, buying prepackaged meals may save time but often comes at a premium price without delivering equivalent value. Wasting money is often characterized by a lack of awareness regarding the true cost of purchases and the long-term impact of these decisions on one's financial health.

Overspending. In contrast, overspending occurs when individuals exceed their budgetary limits, leading to debt accumulation and financial stress. This behavior is frequently driven by emotional factors, societal pressures, or a lack of awareness about one's financial situation. For instance, impulse buying during sales events or feeling compelled to purchase luxury items to maintain a certain lifestyle can lead to overspending. Unlike wasting money, which may not always involve exceeding a budget, overspending explicitly refers to spending beyond one's means. Understanding these definitions is essential for recognizing how both behaviors can negatively impact overall financial health. While wasting money may seem less severe than overspending at first glance, both can contribute to significant financial strain over time.

Psychological Factors

The psychological triggers behind wasting and overspending are complex and multifaceted. A deep understanding of these factors is essential for designing interventions that effectively address these behaviors.

1. **Emotional Spending**. Many individuals engage in emotional spending as a way to cope with feelings of sadness, boredom, or stress. Shopping provides a temporary sense of happiness or distraction from negative emotions. For example, someone might buy new clothes after a tough day at work as a form of self-soothing. While occasional emotional spending may not be

harmful, it could become problematic when it leads to habitual overspending or wasteful purchases.

2. **Impulse Buying**. Often fueled by immediate satisfaction and the thrill of acquiring something new. Retailers exploit this tendency through marketing strategies that create urgency such as limited-time offers or flash sales encouraging consumers to make quick purchasing decisions without considering their budget or needs. The rush associated with impulse buying may lead individuals to overlook the long-term consequences of their spending choices.

3. **Social Influence.** Social pressures significantly impact spending behavior. Individuals may feel compelled to spend money on social activities or gifts for others in order to gain approval or fit in with their peers. For instance, paying for an expensive dinner out with friends might lead to feelings of camaraderie but may also result in overspending that strains one's finances.

4. **Fear of Missing Out (FOMO)**. The fear of missing out on experiences or trends can drive individuals to make hasty purchases. This psychological phenomenon is particularly prevalent in the age of social media, where

curated images of luxury lifestyles create unrealistic expectations about what one should be able to afford. This fear might produce people to spend beyond their means in an attempt to keep up with perceived social norms.

5. **Lack of Financial Literacy**. A fundamental lack of understanding regarding budgeting and financial management may contribute to both wasting and overspending behaviors. Many individuals are not taught essential financial skills during their formative years, leading them to maneuver adult life without the necessary tools for making informed decisions about money.

6. **Cognitive Dissonance**. When individuals make purchases that contradict their financial goals or values, they may experience cognitive dissonance- a psychological discomfort arising from holding conflicting beliefs or attitudes. To alleviate this discomfort, they may rationalize their spending by downplaying its impact on their overall financial health.

Chapter 2
The True Cost of Wasting Money

In the pursuit of financial stability, learning the true cost of wasting money is paramount. This chapter looks into the various dimensions of wasteful spending, identifying common areas where waste occurs, examining its impact on overall financial health, and presenting real-life case studies that illustrate the consequences of such behaviors. Through recognizing the hidden costs associated with wasteful spending, readers may take actionable steps toward more mindful financial practices.

Identifying Wasteful Spending

Wasteful spending could manifest in numerous ways across different aspects of life. Knowing these areas is vital for mitigating waste and enhancing financial health.

1. **Groceries**

    One of the most significant areas where waste occurs is in grocery shopping. Ample individuals buy items they do not need or fail to consume perishable goods before they spoil. According to the Food and Agriculture Organization (FAO), approximately one-third of all food produced globally is wasted, translating to billions of dollars lost each year. Strategies such as meal planning, creating shopping lists, and using apps to track expiration dates could also help reduce this type of waste.

2. Utilities

Utility bills normally reflect wasteful spending habits that go unnoticed. For example, leaving lights on in unoccupied rooms, overusing heating or cooling systems, and neglecting to turn off appliances may lead to inflated energy bills. Simple changes, like using energy-efficient bulbs or smart thermostats, also significantly reduce utility expenses.

3. Subscriptions

In today's digital age, it is easy to accumulate multiple subscriptions for streaming services, magazines, and apps. Many people subscribe to services they rarely use or forget about entirely. A study by the financial technology company *Truebill* found that Americans waste over $200 billion annually on unused subscriptions. Regularly reviewing subscription services and canceling those that are underutilized can free up significant funds.

4. Impulse Purchases

Impulse buying is another common source of wasteful spending. Often driven by emotional triggers or marketing tactics, these purchases can lead to buyer's remorse and financial strain. Implementing a "cooling-off" period waiting 24 hours before making non-essential purchases help curb impulse buying tendencies.

5. **Convenience Items**

While convenience products save time, they always come at a premium price. Pre-cut vegetables, ready-to-eat meals, and single serving snacks may be convenient but lead to unnecessary expenditures over time. Preparing meals from scratch and buying in bulk will yield significant savings.

Impact on Financial Health

The cumulative effect of wasting money could be detrimental to overall financial health:

1. **Decreased Savings**

Money wasted on unnecessary items directly reduces the funds available for savings and investments. This lack of savings hinder individuals from building an emergency fund or preparing for retirement.

2. **Increased Debt**

Wasteful spending usually leads individuals to rely on credit cards or loans to cover essential expenses when their budget is stretched too thin. This cycle of borrowing would also result in accumulating debt and high-interest payments that further exacerbate financial instability.

3. Missed Opportunities

Resources spent on wasteful purchases could have been allocated toward more productive endeavors such as education, skill development, or investments that yield long-term benefits.

4. Stress and Anxiety

Financial waste might contribute to feelings of stress and anxiety as individuals leverage with their financial situation. The constant worry about money affect mental health and overall well-being.

Case Studies

To illustrate the consequences of wasteful spending, consider the following real-life examples:

1. The Grocery Gambit

Sarah, a busy professional, regularly found herself purchasing groceries without a plan. She would buy various items on impulse during her weekly shopping trips but frequently ended up throwing away spoiled food at the end of each week. After tracking her expenses for a month, she realized she was wasting nearly $150 monthly on groceries alone due to spoilage and unused items. By implementing meal planning and creating shopping list based on her needs, Sarah reduced her grocery bill by 30%, freeing up funds for savings.

2. Utility Waste

John lived in a large home but many times left lights on throughout the day and neglected to adjust his thermostat during seasonal changes. His monthly utility bill averaged $400-a figure he considered normal until he began tracking his energy usage with a smart meter app. After making small changes like using LED bulbs and setting his thermostat more efficiently, John reduced his utility costs by 25%, saving $100 each month.

3. Subscription Overload

Emily had subscribed to several streaming services but rarely watched them all due to her busy schedule. When she reviewed her bank statements, she discovered she was paying over

$50 monthly for subscriptions that she barely used. After canceling two services and downgrading another, she saved $30 per month, money she redirected toward her student loan payments.

4. Impulse Buying

Mark frequently succumbed to impulse purchases while shopping online during sales events. He justified these purchases as "treats" for himself but later found he had accumulated items he didn't need or use, totaling nearly $300 over three months. Through implementing a 24-hour waiting period before making online purchases. Mark significantly reduced his impulse buying and reverted those funds toward savings.

Chapter 3
The Danger of Overspending

Overspending is a pervasive issue that affects individuals and families across various socioeconomic backgrounds. It lead to a cycle of debt, stress, and long-term financial repercussions that may take years to recover from. This chapter explores the concept of overspending, the factors that contribute to this behavior, its consequences on financial health, and real-life case studies that illustrate its impact.

Understanding Overspending

Overspending occurs when individuals spend more than they earn or exceed their budgetary limits. This behavior stem from various motivations, including emotional triggers, societal pressures, and a lack of financial awareness. While occasional overspending may not have immediate consequences, habitual overspending could lead to severe financial distress.

Key Characteristics of Overspending:
   a. ***Living Beyond Means***. Regularly spending more than one earns.
   b. ***Relying on Credit***. Using credit cards or loans to cover everyday expenses.
   c. ***Impulse Purchases***. Making unplanned purchases driven by emotions or marketing tactics.
   d. ***Failure to Budget***. Not tracking income and expenses effectively.

Understanding these characteristics is essential for recognizing when spending habits become detrimental.

Factors Leading to Overspending

Several factors contribute to overspending behaviors:

1. **Lifestyle Inflation**

    As individuals experience increases in income, they usually feel compelled to upgrade their lifestyle buying luxury items, moving to more expensive homes, or dining out more frequently. While enjoying the fruits of one's labor is natural excessive lifestyle inflation leads to overspending if not managed carefully.

2. **Peer Pressure**

    Social influences have an important role in spending habits. Friends and family may inadvertently encourage overspending through social activities or expectations. For instance, going out for dinner with friends may lead an individual to spend more than they intended simply to fit in or jeep up with peers.

3. Emotional Triggers

Many people turn to shopping as a way to cope with negative emotions such as stress, anxiety, or boredom. This emotional spending will provide temporary relief but commonly results in regret and financial strain later on.

4. Marketing Tactics

Retailers employ various strategies to entice consumers into spending more. Limited-time offers, sales events, and targeted advertising create a sense of urgency that lead individuals to make impulsive purchases without considering their budget.

5. Lack of Financial Literacy

A fundamental lack of understanding regarding budgeting and financial management could contribute to overspending. Many individuals are not equipped with the necessary skills to manage their finances effectively, leading to make uninformed spending decisions.

6. Boredom and Lack of Planning

Engaging in retail therapy out of boredom or failing to plan purchases would result in unnecessary expenditures. Without a clear plan for spending, individuals may find themselves making impulsive choices that do not align with their financial goals.

Consequences of Overspending

The consequences of overspending extend beyond immediate financial strain, they can have far-reaching implications on an individual's overall well-being:

1. Debt Accumulation

One of the most significant dangers of overspending is the ***accumulation of debt***. When individuals rely on credit cards or loans to cover their expenses, they enter a cycle where debt becomes increasingly difficult to manage. High-interest rates on credit cards led to ballooning debt levels that take years to pay off.

2. Increased Stress and Anxiety

Financial stress is a common consequence of overspending. The constant worry about money results to anxiety and depression, affecting mental health and overall quality of life. Individuals may find it challenging to focus on other aspects of life when burdened by financial worries.

3. **Damaged Credit Score**

Overspending has negatively impact credit scores due to high credit utilization ratios and missed payments. A damaged credit score makes it difficult for individuals to secure loans for essential purchases like homes or cars and it result in higher-interest rates when borrowing.

4. **Strained Relationships**

Money issues generally led to conflicts within relationships whether with partners, family members, or friends. Arguments over finances could create tension and erode trust among loved ones.

5. **Limited Financial Freedom**

Overspending restricts individuals' ability to save for future goals such as retirement, home ownership, or education. When funds are consistently directed toward paying off debt rather than building savings, achieving long-term financial stability becomes increasingly challenging.

6. **Health Consequences**

The stress associated with financial difficulties can manifest physically through sleep disorders, high blood pressure, and other health issues. Additionally, individuals may neglect their health by cutting back on essential services like gym memberships or healthcare due to financial constraints.

Case Studies

To illustrate the impact of overspending on individuals lives, consider the following relatable stories:

1. **The Lifestyle Upgrade Trap**

Jessica received a promotion at work that came with a significant salary increase. Excited about her newfound income, she upgraded her apartment and began dining out frequently with friends. Initially enjoying her new lifestyle, Jessica soon found herself struggling financially as her expenses skyrocketed beyond her income level. Within months, she accumulated over $10,000 in credit card debt due to her inability to maintain her previous budget while indulging in luxury living.

2. **Peer Pressure Pitfall**

Tom continually felt pressured by his friends to participate in expensive outings-dining at upscale restaurants and attending costly events. Despite being on a tight budget as a recent college graduate, he frequently caved into peer pressure and spent beyond his means just to fit in with his social circle. Over time, Tom realized he had drained his savings account and racked up significant credit card debt due to his desire for social acceptance.

3. Emotional Spending Cycle

After experiencing a breakup, Lisa turned to shopping as a way to cope with her feelings of sadness and loneliness. She frequently bought clothes and accessories she didn't need as a form of self-soothing but quickly found herself overwhelmed by guilt when reviewing her bank statements each month. This emotional spending led Lisa into a cycle where she relied on credit cards for everyday expenses until she was unable to make minimum payments resulting in increased stress and anxiety about her financial situation.

4. Boredom-Induced Spending

Mark usually found himself bored during weekends without plans or activities lined up. To fill this void, he began visiting shopping mall and online stores out of sheer boredom making impulse purchases that added up over time without providing lasting satisfaction. Eventually realizing he had spent thousands on items he never used or wore, Mark recognized the need for better planning and budgeting strategies.

Chapter 4
Identifying Personal Spending Traps

In the journey toward financial health, one of the most critical steps is recognizing and addressing personal spending traps. These traps could led to unnecessary expenditures that derail budgets and create financial stress. This chapter will investigate common spending traps such as impulse buying, convenience purchases, and emotional spending. Additionally, it will provide self-assessment tools to help readers identify their spending habits and develop strategies for improvement.

Common Spending Traps

Understanding the various types of spending traps is essential for anyone looking to take control of their finances. Below are some of the most prevalent traps that will lead individuals to waste money:

1. **Impulse Buying**

    Impulse buying occurs when individuals make unplanned purchases without considering their budget or needs. This behavior is always triggered by emotional states, marketing tactics, or simply the excitement of shopping. For example, a shopper might see a "limited-time offer" on a product they don't need and make an impulsive decision to buy it. According to research, impulse purchases can account for a significant portion of consumer spending, regularly leading to buyer's remorse and regret.

2. **Convenience Purchases**

    Convenience purchases are made when individuals opt for quick and easy options that normally come at a premium price. For instance, buying pre-cut vegetables or ready-to-eat meals may save time but typically costs more than preparing food from scratch. This type of spending is particularly prevalent in grocery shopping, where consumers may pay extra for items that require minimal preparation.

3. Emotional Spending

This refers to purchasing items as a way to cope with feelings such as stress, sadness, or boredom. Many people turn to shopping as a form of self-soothing or celebration. While treating oneself occasionally be harmless, habitual emotional spending could result to financial strain and regret when the initial joy from the purchase fades.

4. Social Pressure

The desire to fit in with peers can lead to overspending on social activities or luxury items that one cannot afford. Whether it's dining out at expensive restaurants or participating in costly vacations with friends, social pressures significantly impact spending habits.

5. Discount and Sale Addiction

Many consumers fall into the trap of buying items simply because they are on sale, regardless of whether they need them. The allure of discounts result to individuals to accumulate unnecessary items that clutter their homes and drain their bank accounts.

6. **Subscription Services**

The convenience of subscription services ranging from streaming platforms to meal kits may cause individuals to sign up for multiple services without fully utilizing them. Many people forget about these subscriptions after initial sign-ups, resulting in wasted money each month.

Self-Assessment Tools

To help readers identify their personal spending habits and recognize potential traps, this section provides self-assessment tools in the form of worksheets and quizzes.

Spending Habit Questionnaire

1. How often do you make unplanned purchases?
   A) Rarely
   B) Sometimes
   C) Often
   D) Always

2. Do you usually stick to a shopping list when grocery shopping?

    A) Always

    B) Usually

    C) Sometimes

    D) Never

3. How do you feel after making an impulse purchase?

    A) Happy

    B) Neutral

    C) Regretful

    D) Guilty

4. Do you frequently buy items on sale that you don't need?

    A) Never

    B) Rarely

    C) Sometimes

    D) Often

5. How often do you spend money to cope with stress or negative emotions?

    A) Never

B) Rarely

C) Sometimes

D) Often

Scoring System:

For each "A," give yourself 1 point.

For each "B," give yourself 2 points.

For each "C," give yourself 3 points.

For each "D," give yourself 4 points.

Interpretation:

(***5-10 points***) You have a good handle on your spending habits but remain vigilant against potential traps.

(***11-15 points***) You occasionally fall into spending traps, consider implementing stricter budgeting practices.

(***16-20 points***) You may frequently engage in wasteful spending, it's essential to identify specific triggers and develop strategies for improvement.

(***21+ points***) Overspending may be a significant issue, consider seeking financial counseling or support to address these behaviors.

Strategies for Overcoming Spending Traps

Once readers have identified their personal spending habits through self-assessment, they can implement strategies to combat these traps:

1. ***Create a Budget***. Establishing a clear budget helps track income and expenses while prioritizing needs over wants.

2. ***Use Cash for Purchases***. Limiting the use of credit cards might help control impulse buying by making transactions feel more tangible.

3. ***Implement a Waiting Period***. Before making non-essential purchases, consider instituting a waiting period (e.g., 24 hours) to evaluate whether the item is truly needed.

4. ***Be Mindful of Marketing Tactics***. Recognize how retailers use psychological strategies (e.g., FOMO-fear of missing out) to encourage overspending and resist these temptations.

5. ***Limit Exposure to Sales Promotions***. Unsubscribe from promotional emails or avoid browsing sales websites unless actively looking for something specific.

6. ***Engage in Alternative Activities***. Find non-spending activities that provide fulfillment, such as exercising, reading, or pursuing hobbies that don't require financial investment.

3 True Cost of Wasting vs. Overspending

Chapter 5
Strategies to Combat Wastefulness

As individuals seek to improve their financial health, combating wastefulness becomes a critical focus. Wasteful spending may erode savings, lead to debt accumulation, and create unnecessary financial stress. This chapter outlines effective strategies for mindful spending, provides practical tips for reducing waste in daily life, and recommends tools and apps that could help track expenses and monitor spending habits.

Mindful Spending Techniques

Mindful spending is about making intentional choices regarding how and where money is spent. Here are several techniques to acquire mindfulness in financial decisions:

1. **Create a Budget**

Establishing a budget is foundational to mindful spending. A budget outlines income, fixed expenses (like rent or mortgage), variable expenses (like groceries), and savings goals. By categorizing spending, individuals could gain a clearer picture of their financial situation and identify areas where waste may occur.

2. **Practice Meal Planning**

Meal planning not only saves time but also reduces food waste. Through planning meals for the week, individuals may create shopping lists that focus on necessary ingredients, minimizing impulse purchases at the grocery store. This practice helps avoid buying items that may go unused or spoil before consumption.

3. **Implement the 30-Day Rule**

Before making non-essential purchases, consider waiting 30 days. This cooling-off period allows individuals to reflect on whether the item is truly needed or if the desire to purchase was driven by impulse or emotional triggers.

4. Use Cash Instead of Credit

Paying with cash can help individuals become more aware of their spending habits. When using cash, the physical act of handling over money create a more tangible connection to spending, making it easier to stick to a budget.

5. Limit Exposure to Temptations

Reduce exposure to advertisements and shopping temptations by unsubscribing from promotional emails and avoiding browsing online stores unless actively shopping for something specific. This might help minimize impulse buys driven by marketing tactics.

6. Set Clear Financial Goals

Establishing short-term and long-term financial goals could provide motivation for mindful spending. Whether saving for a vacation, a new car, or retirement, having clear goals helps prioritize spending decisions and fosters discipline.

7. Evaluate Subscription Services

Regularly review subscription services to determine which ones are truly beneficial. Cancel any subscriptions that are underutilized or no longer provide value. This simple step might free up funds for more meaningful expenditures.

Tips for Reducing Waste in Daily Life

In addition to mindful spending techniques, there are practical tips that individuals would implement in their daily routines to reduce waste:

1. ***Track Spending Habits***

    Keeping a detailed record of daily expenditures helps identify patterns of wasteful spending. With tracking where money goes each month, individuals might pinpoint areas of improvement.

2. ***Buy in Bulk Wisely***

    Purchasing items in bulk could contribute to savings, however, it's essential to ensure that bulk items will be used before they expire. Buying non-perishable goods or items that are frequently used can be a smart way to save money without creating waste.

3. ***Use Unit Pricing***

When shopping for groceries, pay attention to unit pricing (cost per ounce or pound). this practice helps identify the best deals and avoid overpaying for products.

4. *Plan for Leftovers*

Cooking larger meals intentionally allows for leftovers that could be repurposed into new dishes throughout the week. This not only saves time but also reduces food waste.

5. *Adopt Minimalism*

Embracing a minimalist mindset encourages individuals to focus on quality over quantity when it comes to purchases through prioritizing essential items and reducing clutter, individuals might save money and live more intentionally.

6. *Engage in DIY Projects*

Consider tackling do-it-yourself projects rather than purchasing new items or services whenever possible. Whether it's home repairs or creating gifts, DIY projects remarkably save money while fostering creativity.

Tools and Apps for Tracking Expenses

To support mindful spending and reduce wastefulness, various tools and apps are available that help individuals track expenses and monitor their financial habits effectively:

1. *Mint*

Mint is a free budgeting tool that allows users to track expenses across multiple categories automatically linked to bank accounts and credit cards. It provides insights into spending habits, alerts users about bills due, and offers personalized budgeting recommendations based on individual financial behavior.

2. *YNAB (You Need a Budget)*

This encourages users to allocate every cash they earn toward specific categories (including savings) through its zero-based budgeting approach. The app helps users prioritize their spending based on income while minimizing debt accumulation. YNAB offers a free trial followed by a monthly subscription fee.

3. *GoodBudget*

Utilizes the envelope budgeting system digitally, allowing users to allocate funds into virtual envelopes for various categories (e.g., groceries, entertainment) users manually input their transactions while tracking their remaining balances in each envelope, helping them stay within budget limits.

4. *EveryDollar*

Designed for zero-based budgeting and allows users to manually enter their income and expenses throughout the month easily. The premium version connects bank accounts for automatic transaction tracking, making it easier to monitor finances.

5. *PocketGuard*

This apps simplifies budgeting by showing users how much disposable income they have after accounting for bills, necessities, and savings goals. Users can connect bank accounts for real-time tracking of expenses while maintaining an overview of their financial health.

6. *Wally*

Wally is an expense tracker that allows users to log their income and expenses manually or by scanning receipts directly within the apps. It provides insights into spending patterns while helping users set budgets based on personal financial goals.

7. *Expensify*

Primarily designed for business expense tracking. Expensify allows users to take photos of receipts and categorize expenses easily making it an excellent tool for freelancers or those managing side hustles alongside personal finances.

8. *Mvelopes*

Uses the envelope budgeting method digitally by allowing users to allocate cash into virtual envelopes based on their budget categories preventing overspending in any given area.

9. *Dime*

Another expense tracker app that focuses on manual entry of transactions while providing insights into overall spending habits, helping users identify areas where they may be wasting money.

Chapter 6
Strategies to Control

Overspending

Overspending could result to significant financial distress, making it essential for individuals to develop effective strategies to manage their spending habits. This chapter focuses on two key components creating a sustainable budget that aligns with individual lifestyles and setting financial goals that promote disciplined spending. By implementing these strategies, readers gain better control over their finances and work toward long-term financial stability.

Creating a Sustainable Budget

A well-structured budget serves as a roadmap for managing income and expenses, enabling individuals to make informed financial decisions. Here's how to create a sustainable budget that fits your lifestyle:

1. **Assess Your Income**

Begin by calculating your total monthly income. This includes all sources of revenue, such as salaries, bonuses, side hustles, and any other income streams. Having a clear understanding of your total income is crucial for establishing a realistic budget.

2. **Track Your Expenses**

For at least one month, track all your expenses meticulously. Categorize them into fixed expenses (e.g., rent, utilities) and variable expenses (e.g., groceries, entertainment). this tracking will help you identify spending patterns and areas where you may be overspending.

3. **Choose a Budgeting Method**

There are several budgeting methods to consider:

a. ***Zero-Based Budgeting***. Allocate every funds of your income to specific expenses, savings, or debt repayment, ensuring that your income minus your expenses equals zero at the end of the month.

b. ***50/30/20 Rule***. Allocate 50% of your income to needs (essentials), 30% to wants (discretionary spending), and 20% to savings and debt repayment.

c. ***Envelope System***. Use physical envelopes or digital equivalents for different spending categories. Once the money in an envelope is gone, no more spending is allowed in that category for the month.

4. Set Realistic Spending Limits

Based on your tracked expenses and chosen budgeting method, set realistic spending limits for each category. Ensure that these limits reflect your lifestyle while allowing room for savings and debt repayment.

5. Review and Adjust Regularly

A budget is not static, it should evolve with changes in income, expenses, or financial goals. Review your budget monthly or quarterly to assess its effectiveness and make necessary adjustments.

6. Incorporate Savings into Your Budget

Treat savings as a non-negotiable expense by including it in your budget from the outset. Aim to save at least 20% of your income if possible, directing these funds toward an emergency fund or specific financial goals.

7. **Use Budgeting Tools and Apps**

Leverage technology to simplify budgeting. Apps like *Mint*, *YNAB*, or *GoodBudget* could help automate tracking expenses and managing budgets effectively.

Setting Financial Goals

Setting financial goals is a very important aspect of controlling overspending. Goals provide direction and motivation, helping individuals prioritize their spending decisions. Here's how to effectively set financial goals:

1. **Understand the Importance of Goals**

Financial goals serve as benchmarks for measuring progress and success. They help individuals stay focused on what matters most while reducing the temptation to overspend on non-essential items.

2. **Categorize Your Goals**

   a. ***Short-Term Goals***. These are achievable within one year and may include saving for a vacation, paying off a specific debt, or buying new appliances.

b. ***Mid-Term Goals***. These typically take one to five years to achieve and might include purchasing a car or saving for a home down payment.

c. ***Long-Term Goals***. These require more than five years of planning and commitment, examples include saving for retirement or funding a child's education.

3. Use the SMART Criteria

When setting goals, ensure they are:

- ***Specific***. Clearly define what you want to achieve (e.g., "Save $5,000 for a vacation").

- ***Measurable***. Establish criteria for measuring progress (e.g., "Save $500 each month").

- ***Achievable***. Set realistic goals based on your current financial situation.

- ***Relevant***. Ensure your goals align with your values and long-term aspirations.

- ***Time-Bound***. Set deadlines for achieving each goal (e.g., "Save $5,000 by next summer").

4. Create a Financial Goals Chart

Document your goals in a chart or spreadsheet that outlines each goal's specifics, timeline, required savings amount, and progress tracking. Regularly review this chart to stay accountable.

5. Break Down Larger Goals into Actionable Steps

For more significant financial goals, outline smaller steps needed to achieve them. For example, if saving for a home down payment is a long-term goal, break it down into monthly savings targets based on the total amount needed.

6. Celebrate Milestones

As you achieve short-term or mid-term goals, take time to celebrate these accomplishments. This positive reinforcement can motivate you to continue working toward larger objectives.

7. Adjust Goals as Necessary

Life circumstances change, therefore, be flexible with your financial goals. If you encounter unexpected expenses or change in income, reassess your goals and timeliness accordingly.

Chapter 7
The Role of Consumer Awareness

In an age of information overload and aggressive marketing tactics, consumer awareness is more critical than ever. Understanding how marketing influences spending behavior and educating oneself on the distinction between value and price may empower consumers to make informed financial decisions. This chapter explores the role of consumer awareness in combating wastefulness and overspending, emphasizing the importance of recognizing marketing strategies and differentiating between necessary expenses and luxury items.

Understanding Marketing Strategies

Marketing strategies are designed to influence consumer behavior by promoting products or services that meet specific needs. These strategies encompass a variety of techniques aimed at attracting potential customers and converting them into loyal buyers. Here are key elements that illustrate how marketing influences spending behavior:

1. **Segmentation, Targeting, and Positioning (STP)**

    Successful marketing begins with understanding the target market. Companies segment their audience based on demographics, interests, and behaviors to tailor their messaging effectively. Through specific customer segments, businesses can create targeted campaigns that resonate with potential buyers, increasing the likelihood of purchase.

2. **The Four Ps of Marketing**

    The four Ps (Product, Price, Place, and Promotion) are foundational elements of any marketing strategy:

    a. ***Product***. This refers to the goods or services offered to satisfy customer needs. Marketers work to ensure that their products stand out in a crowded marketplace.

    b. ***Price***. Pricing strategies can significantly influence consumer perception. Consumers often associate higher prices with higher quality, leading them to spend more on perceived luxury items.

c. ***Place***. This refers to the distribution channels through which product are sold. Accessibility takes the lead role in consumer purchasing decisions, if a product is easy to find or purchase online, consumers are more likely to buy it.

   d. ***Promotion***. Promotional tactics include advertising, public relations, social media campaigns, and sales promotions that create awareness and drive consumer interest.

3. Emotional Appeals

Many marketing campaigns leverage emotional triggers to influence purchasing decisions. Advertisements often evoke feelings such as nostalgia, happiness, or fear of missing out (FOMO) to encourage consumers to buy products they may not read.

4. Social Proof

Consumers are heavily influenced by the opinions and behaviors of others. Marketing strategies often incorporate testimonials, reviews, or influencer endorsements to build trust and credibility around a product or service.

5. Scarcity and Urgency

Marketers frequently create a sense of urgency by promoting limited-time offers or low stock levels. This tactic encourages consumers to make quick purchasing decisions out of fear that they might miss out on a great deal.

6. **Brand Loyalty**

Successful marketing strategies foster brand loyalty through consistent messaging and positive customer experiences. When consumers feel connected to a brand, they are more likely to make repeat purchases even at higher price points.

Educating Yourself on Value vs. Price

Understanding the difference between value and price is essential for making informed financial choices:

1. **Defining Value**

Value refers to the perceived benefit derived from a product or service relative to its cost. It encompasses not only monetary aspects but also factors such as quality, durability, convenience, and emotional satisfaction. A high-value product offers significant benefits that justify its price.

2. Understanding Price

Price is the amount of money required to purchase a product or service. While price is an important consideration in purchasing decisions, it does not always reflect the true value of an item.

3. Evaluating Necessity vs. Luxury

a. ***Necessary Expenses.*** These are essential expenditures required for basic living such as housing, utilities, groceries, transportation, and healthcare. When budgeting, it's important to prioritize these necessary expenses.

b. ***Luxury Items.*** Luxury items are non-essential goods that enhance comfort or status but do not contribute directly to survival or well-being (e.g., designer clothing, high-end electronics). while these items can provide enjoyment, it's requisite for consumers to evaluate whether such purchases align with their financial goals.

4. Cost-Benefit Analysis

Before making a purchase decision especially for higher-priced items, conducting a cost-benefit analysis can help clarify whether the expense is justified based on its value proposition.

5. **Researching Alternatives**

Educated consumers should research alternatives before making purchases. Comparing similar products across different brands can reveal better value options that may be less expensive but still meet needs effectively.

6. **Avoiding Impulse Purchases**

Being aware of marketing tactics help consumers resist impulsive buying decisions driven by emotional appeals or promotional pressure. Taking time to reflect on whether an item aligns with personal values could also prevent unnecessary expenditures.

Chapter 8
Building Healthy Financial Habits

Establishing healthy financial habits is essential for achieving long-term financial stability and success. In this chapter, we will explore practical strategies for creating routines that support financial health, the importance of accountability in maintaining discipline, and how sharing financial goals with friends or family could enhance commitment to those goals.

Establishing Routines for Financial Success

Creating a structured approach to managing finances involves developing daily, weekly, and monthly practices that promote awareness and control over spending. Here are some effective routines that help individuals maintain their financial health.

1. **Daily Practices**

a. ***Track Daily Expenses***. Make it a habit to record every expense, no matter how small. This practice increases awareness of spending patterns and helps identify areas where waste may occur. Use a notebook, spreadsheet, or budgeting app to log daily expenditures.

b. ***Review Financial Goals***. Spend a few minutes each day reflecting on your financial goals. Whether saving for a vacation or paying off debt, visualizing these objectives could reinforce your commitment to mindful spending.

c. ***Limit Impulse Purchases***. Before making any unplanned purchases, pause and assess whether the item aligns with your financial goals. Implementing a brief waiting period (e.g., 24 hours) before making non-essential purchases may help curb impulsive buying.

2. **Weekly Practices**
    a. ***Budget Review***. Set aside time each week to review your budget. Compare actual spending against your planned budget and adjust as necessary. This practice helps ensure you stay on track and identify any overspending trends early.

    b. ***Meal Planning***. Dedicate time each week to plan meals and create a grocery list based on those plans. This reduces food waste and helps control grocery spending by focusing on necessary items.

c. ***Check-in with Financial Goals***. Assess progress toward your short-term and long-term financial goals weekly. Celebrate small victories, such as reaching a savings milestone or successfully sticking to your budget.

3. **Monthly Practices**

   a. ***Comprehensive Financial Review***. Conduct a thorough review of your finances at the end of each month. Analyze income, expenses, savings, and debt repayment progress. This allows you to make informed decisions about adjustments needed for the upcoming month.
   b. ***Adjust Budget as Necessary***. Based on your monthly review, update your budget to reflect any changes in income or expenses. If you notice consistent overspending in certain categories, consider revising those limits or finding ways to cut back.
   c. **Plan for Upcoming Expenses**. Anticipate any significant expenses in the coming month (e.g., bills, events) and incorporate them into your budget. Planning ahead helps avoid surprises that could lead to overspending.

The Importance of Accountability

Accountability is a vital component of building healthy financial habits. When individuals hold themselves accountable for their financial decisions, they are more likely to stay disciplined and committed to their goals.

Accountability involves taking responsibility for one's actions and decisions regarding finances. It fosters transparency in spending habits and encourages individuals to evaluate their choices critically.

Benefits of Accountability

a. ***Enhanced Discipline.*** Knowing that someone else is aware of your financial goals can motivate you to stick to them. Accountability partners also provide encouragement during challenging times and celebrate successes together.

b. ***Increased Motivation.*** Sharing financial goal with others creates a support system that boost motivation. When you have someone cheering you on or checking in on your progress, it reinforces your commitment to achieving those goals.

c. ***Reduced Isolation***. Discussing financial challenges with friends or family may alleviate feelings of isolation oftentimes associated with money management struggles. It opens up conversations about shared experiences and strategies for overcoming obstacles.

Finding an Accountability Partner

 a. ***Choose Wisely***. Select someone who shares similar values regarding finances or has experience managing their own finances effectively. This could be a friend, family member, or even a mentor.

 b. ***Set Regular Check-Ins***. Schedule regular meetings (weekly or monthly) with your accountability partner to discuss progress toward your financial goals. Use this time to share successes, challenges, and strategies for improvement.

Consider participating in financial workshops or support groups where members share their experiences and hold each other accountable for achieving their financial objectives.

Chapter 9

Case Studies and Success Stories

In the journey toward financial health, real-life transformations serve as powerful motivators and practical examples of how individuals successfully reduce waste and overspending. This chapter highlights several profiles of individuals who have made significant changes in their financial habits, illustrating the strategies they employed and the lessons learned along the way. These success stories demonstrate that with determination, education, and the right tools, anyone could achieve their financial goals.

Real-Life Transformations

1. Sarah's Journey to Financial Freedom

Sarah, a 32-year-old marketing professional, found herself living paycheck despite earning a decent salary. She frequently indulged in impulse purchases, particularly clothing and dining out, which led to mounting credit card debt. Realizing that her spending habits were unsustainable, Sarah decided to take control of her finances. She began by tracking her expenses using a budgeting app and quickly identified that she was spending over $400 a month on dining out and $300 on clothing.

With this, Sarah created a zero-based budget, allocating every dollar of her income to specific expenses and savings goals. She started meal prepping for the week, significantly reducing her grocery bills and eliminating the temptation to eat out. To combat impulse buying, Sarah implemented a 30-day rule for non-essential purchases, allowing her time to consider whether she truly needed the item.

Within six months, Sarah paid off $5,000 in credit card debt and saved an additional $2,000 for an emergency fund. Her newfound financial awareness not only alleviated stress but also allowed her to enjoy life without the burden of debt.

2. **Mark's Minimalist Approach**

Mark, a 28-year-old software engineer, was overwhelmed by clutter and unnecessary expenses. He realized that his possessions were not bringing him happiness but rather stress and financial strain. Inspired by minimalism, Mark decided to clear out his life both physically and financially. He recognized that his spending habits were closely tied to his emotional well-being.

He went through his belongings and sold or donated items he no longer used or needed. This process not only cleared physical space but also provided him with extra cash. He adopted a minimalist mindset when it came to purchasing new items, focusing on quality over quantity. Mark set strict limits on discretionary spending each month. He also established clear financial goals, including saving for travel experiences rather than material possessions.

After one year, Mark had saved enough money for a three-month trip abroad while maintaining a clutter-free home. His focus on experiences over things brought him greater joy and fulfillment.

3. **Emily's Debt-Free Journey**

Emily was a recent college graduate with significant student loan debt. She struggled to manage her finances while trying to enjoy her new career and social life. Frustrated by her debt situation, Emily sought advice from a financial coach who helped her develop a plan to tackle her loans while still enjoying life.

Due to this, Emily prioritized paying off her smallest debts first while making minimum payments on larger ones. This strategy provided her quick wins that motivated her to continue. To accelerate her debt repayment, Emily took on freelance work in addition to her full-time job. She dedicated all extra income toward paying off loans. Also, she created a budget that included fun money for social activities without derailing her debt repayment plan.

Within two years, Emily paid off $25,000 in student loans. She learned valuable lessons about budgeting and prioritizing financial goals while still enjoying life's pleasures.

4. Tom's Family Financial Overhaul

Tom and his wife struggled with overspending as they tried to provide for their two children while managing household expenses. They often found themselves in debt due to unplanned purchases and lifestyle inflation. After attending a financial literacy workshop at their local community center, Tom realized they needed a comprehensive plan to regain control over their finances.

Owing to their condition, Tom and his wife held weekly family meetings to discuss their budget and spending priorities as a team. This open communication helped them align their financial goals. They implemented monthly savings challenges where the family would collectively decide on areas to cut back (e.g., entertainment or dining out) and save the difference for family activities or vacations. They involved their children in discussions about money management, teaching them the importance of saving and budgeting from an early age.

Over three years, Tom's family reduced their overall spending by 30% while increasing their savings rate significantly. They managed to pay off credit card debt and save for their children's education.

5. **Jessica's Waste Reduction Initiative**

Jessica was concerned about both her personal finances and environmental impact due to excessive waste generation in her household. As a mother of three, she wanted to create a more sustainable lifestyle while saving money. After learning about zero-waste living through social media influences and documentaries, Jessica decided to make significant changes in how her family consumed goods.

To this end, Jessica invested in reusable products such as water bottles, cloth shopping bags, and beeswax wraps instead of plastic wraps. This not only reduced waste but also saved money over time by avoiding single-use products. She began shopping at bulk stores where she could buy grains, nuts, and cleaning supplies without excessive packaging. This practice significantly cut down on waste while lowering grocery costs. Jessica started composting food scraps from meal preparation instead of throwing them away. This practice not only reduced landfill contributions but also provided nutrient-rich compost for her garden.

Within a year, Jessica reported that her family had reduced waste by 50% and saved approximately $100 per month on groceries by adopting these sustainable practices.

Conclusion

As we reach the end of *"True Cost of Wasting vs. Overspending: A Guide to Smart Financial Choices,"* it is essential to reflect on the key takeaways from this journey toward financial awareness and empowerment. Throughout this book, we have explored the intricacies of personal finance, focusing on the critical distinctions between wasting money and overspending, and how these behaviors can significantly impact our financial health.

We began by defining the concepts of wasting money and overspending. Wasting money often involves expenditures that provide little to no value, while overspending refers to exceeding one's budgetary limits, leading to debt accumulation. Recognizing these behaviors is the first step toward making informed financial decisions.

We examined common spending traps such as impulse buying, convenience purchases, and emotional spending. By identifying these traps, readers can develop strategies to avoid unnecessary expenditures and acquire mindful spending habits.

The book provided practical techniques for reducing waste in daily life, including ,meal planning, budgeting, and utilizing tools and apps for tracking expenses. These strategies empower individuals to take control of their finances and make conscious spending choices.

We discussed the importance of creating a sustainable budget that aligns with individual lifestyles and setting clear financial goals. Through prioritizing necessary expenses and distinguishing between needs and wants, individuals can curb overspending behaviors effectively.

Understanding marketing strategies and educating oneself on the difference between value and price is crucial for making informed purchasing decisions. Increased consumer awareness helps individuals resist impulsive buying driven by emotional triggers or marketing tactics.

Establishing routines for financial success through daily, weekly, and monthly practices fosters discipline in managing finances. Additionally, accountability whether through sharing goals with friends or family, can enhance commitment to achieving financial objectives.

The case studies highlighted in this book illustrated that positive change is possible through determination and effective strategies. These stories serve as inspiration for readers seeking to improve their financial situations.

As you close this book, remember that the journey toward better financial health is not a sprint but a marathon. It requires patience, persistence, and a willingness to learn from both successes and setbacks. The insights shared within these pages are not merely theoretical, they are actionable steps that can lead to meaningful change in your financial life.

Embrace the knowledge you have gained about managing wastefulness and overspending. Take the time to assess your current spending habits honesty, identify areas for improvement, and implement the strategies discussed throughout this book. Remember that every small step counts-whether it's creating a budget, tracking your expenses, or setting clear financial goals.

Change may feel daunting at times, but it is essential to recognize that you have the power to shape your financial future. Surround yourself with supportive individuals who encourage your growth and hold you accountable for your goals. Celebrate your achievements along the way, no matter how small and use them as motivation to continue striving for improvement,

In conclusion, let this book serve as a catalyst for positive change in your life. By taking control of your finances and making informed choices about spending, you can reduce wastefulness, curb overspending, and ultimately achieve greater financial stability and peace of mind. The journey may require effort and dedication, but the rewards will be well worth it, a more secure future where you can focus on what truly matters in life.

Thank you for joining me on this journey toward smarter financial choices! Embrace the path ahead with confidence and determination, your future self will thank you for it.

Appendices

A. Resources for Further Reading
1. Books

- "*The Total Money Makeover*" by Dave Ramsey. A step-by-step guide to financial fitness emphasizes budgeting, saving, and debt elimination.

- "*Your Money or Your Life*" by Vicki Robin and Joe Dominguez. This book offers a foundational approach to money management, focusing on aligning spending with personal values.

- "*The Simple Path to Wealth*" by JL Collins. A straightforward guide to investing and building wealth, emphasizing the importance of financial independence.

- "*I Will Teach You to Be Rich*" by Ramit Sethi. A practical guide aimed at millennials that covers budgeting, saving, and investing in a relatable manner.

2. Articles

- ***NerdWallet.*** Offers a wealth of articles on budgeting, saving, and managing debt. Visit NerdWallet for tips and tools.

- ***The Balance.*** Provides comprehensive guides on various personal finance topics, including budgeting strategies and financial planning. Explore articles at The Balance.

- ***Investopedia.*** A great source for understanding financial concepts and investment strategies. Check out their educational content at Investopedia.

3. Websites

- ***Mint.*** An online budgeting tool that helps users track expenses and create budgets. Access it at Mint.

- ***YNAB (You Need A Budget).*** a budgeting app designed to help users take control of their finances through proactive budgeting practices. Learn more at YNAB.

- ***Vertex42***. Offers a variety of free Excel templates for budgeting and expense tracking. Visit Vertex42 for downloadable templates.

B. Worksheets and Templates

1. Monthly Expense Tracker
- Use this template to record your daily spending across various categories. This will help you identify patterns in your spending habits.

- Download a customizable version from ***https://nomoredebts.org/financial-*** *education/monthly-expense-tracker.*

2. Budget Templates
- **Zero-Based Budget Worksheet**. Allocate every dollar of your income to specific expenses or savings goals. Download it from *https://www.vertex42.com/search.html?q=zero-based+budget+worksheet.*

- **Personal Monthly Budget Worksheet**. Track your income and expenses monthly with this straightforward template available at *https://www.smartsheet.com/content/monthly-budget-template-google-sheets.*

3. Savings Goal Tracker

- Keep track of your savings goals and monitor progress toward achieving them with this simple template.

- Find a downloadable version at

    https://www.nerdwallet.com/article/finance/free-*budget-spreadsheets-templates*

4. Expense Tracking Worksheet

- This worksheet allows you to categorize your expenses and analyze where your money is going each month.

- Access a printable version from

    https://learn.tearfund.org/en/resources/footsteps/footsteps-71-80/footsteps*-76/financial-accountability*

5. Weekly Budget Template

- Use this template to gain a detailed view of your weekly income and expenditures, helping you identify trends in your spending habits.

- Download it from

    https://www.smartsheet.com/content/monthly-budget-template- *google-sheets#weekly-budget-template*

6. Cash Flow Statement Template

- Track your cash flow on a monthly basis with this customizable template that helps you visualize income versus expenses.

- Find it at

    https://www.vertex42.com/ExcelTemplates/cash-flow-statement.html.

About the Author

Avan B. Maamo

Avan Maamo is a dedicated public school teacher with over eight years of experience. His passion for reading and writing has been a lifelong pursuit, fueling his desire to explore various subjects through books, literature, and journals. This passion has led him to create and publish his debut book, "Why Discipline Matters: Why We Need It and How It Transforms Lives."

Available for purchase and online viewing, "Why Discipline Matters: Why We Need It and How It Transforms Lives" is a testament to Avan's commitment to helping others. driven by a genuine desire to make a positive impact, he aims to provide individuals with valuable insights and practical guidance to handle life's challenges. Regardless facing financial difficulties, spiritual uncertainties, emotional turmoil, family problems, or personal development roadblocks, Avan believes that discipline is a fundamental key to overcoming adversity.

www.ingramcontent.com/pod-product-compliance
Lightning Source LLC
LaVergne TN
LVHW041629070526
838199LV00052B/3286